Safe Thus Far

Journeys Through Beauty and Brokenness

Fred Swartz

PublishAmerica
Baltimore

Hardcover 978-1-4512-1211-2
Softcover 978-1-4512-1212-9
PUBLISHED BY PUBLISHAMERICA, LLLP
www.publishamerica.com
Baltimore

Printed in the United States of America

Acknowledgements

First, my gratitude goes to the Lord Jesus Christ, without whom nothing is beautiful.
Next, to my wife, Lacey, who has borne much brokenness with grace and love.
Third, to the brothers at Denny's and in Westmont who taught me how to fight for who God made me to be.
Fourth and finally to the many who have helped me begin laboring for something bigger than myself, some without even knowing it.

Contents

Brokenness

Safe Thus Far
(Psalm 139, II Corinthians 12)

The first shadows of memory are dim indeed—
So distant from where you have brought me
And yet the foundation for much of what you have done
in me.
Even fear and rejection,
Those foulest capstones of fallen man,
Were well-used instruments in your skillful hands.
They have been fire and furnace to fashion my heart
Long before I ever could name them.

Fear I first found at water's edge
As I was tossed thoughtlessly into a bottomless depth,
And it has stayed with me.
For many depths there are in my heart
That still cause me to quake at the thought of plumbing
them.

Rejection hatched in a lunchroom quarrel,
Doubtless over something small
But large enough to teach me I wasn't liked.
And then it devoured me with thanklessness
That followed a gift given to one unseen.

But life was not all tears and sorrow,
For Lucas, Donruss, Fleer and Topps
Were ample shelters from the brewing storm.
Nearby friends and family
Loved me away from much of the pain
And taught me joy and passion in this life.

Storming the Death Star never grew old,
Nor did Hoth's chill numb me.
The vast domain of ancient ball parks
Gave me room to spread my wings.

And in the shadows you waited through it all,
Not lurking but preparing me
To finally see past myself.
It happened once or twice—
Looking into the mirror and wondering who I saw,
Calling out to one I sensed must be,
But the day of visitation had not yet come.

Soon thereafter a fire you ignited.
Unfair it seemed to be so mocked,
To be outside the lordly ones.
Cool, confident they seemed,
The center of attention.
And how I began to long for that,
For affirmation from the crowd,
For a place where I could belong and be king.
Their venom made them popular.
They knew they ruled the roost
And strutted, feathers out, so that no one would forget it.
Ruling in the name of Cool, that foul idol,
They both dispensed and removed
The status of acceptable.

Back in my cottage fortress my walls grew thick.
Castles and dragons and wizards
Joined the throng of Teenage Mutant Masters of the GI
Jedi Universe,

Brandishing lightsabers and katanas to ward off the hurt,
Brimstone breath and arcane lightning
Incinerating every advancing pang.

I was running harder than ever,
Hiding in closets, dungeons, 8-bit shelters,
And locker rooms of pennant winners that never were,
Still not knowing what phantom pursued me.

It was then you nearly had me cornered.
My marrow mourned and moaned within,
Crying for deliverance from something cruel but still
nameless.
The tyrant kings of adolescence
Would daily boast of carnal conquests.
The locker room was podium to a thousand sordid tales,
While I listened silently,
Jealously watching their egos swell.

It was no sensitive crush nor even base lust
With which I next wrought my heartless chains,
But with a hollow heart that longed to be filled.
Surely if the lords of puberty
Found their worth in fleshly feasts,
Then I, the geek, the dork,
Uncool beyond all hope of love,
Could find just a shred of merit and praise
In viewing on paper and film the conquests of others.
Long in that barren waste did I search for that scrap,
Longer than I ever wanted.

And there you finally found me —
Shriveled, withered, dead as stone,

A pile of dust and bone, reeking of decay.
You gave me a voice to cry out to you.
You gave me eyes to see the thick darkness enveloping me.
You opened my heart to finally feel the pain
And quickened me so I could run to you at last.
Had it not been so dark and so cold
I doubt I would have heard your call.
Great is your wisdom and patience,
For you bore my rebellion so long.

The credits had rolled on episode I.
Now outwardly at least I walked confidently.
The princes of youth had lost their crowns.
No more did they terrify,
For I saw how great and glorious you are.
You gave me worth and hope and peace,
So long absent from my heart and soul

And yet longings never die,
Only perhaps transmute to something new,
More complicated and perplexing than before
For still companionship eluded me.
The gentle touch of mortal love,
That highest virtue of poetic art,
Deftly dodged my dogged pursuit,
Making stronger the shackles of lust,
Stunting growth and clouding vision of my Holy One,
My Consuming Fire,
My Ever-present Help,
So you pressed the chase
Past bulwarks of doubt and fear,
Over palisades of arrogance

Meant to keep my heart secure,
Through a wilderness of pain and hurt,
As presumption turned to faith
And weakness into strength,
And a self-styled lord into one willing to serve

You taught me how to love those who curse you,
To live honestly in a world at war.
You showed me passion in my depths
To open minds and challenge hearts.
You taught me how to love a woman,
Not tempestuously in hormonal frenzy,
But from my heart with no agenda,
To hear her fears and joys,
Her hopes and dreams,
And to privilege her to so the same for me.
You have shaped me, Master Potter.
Still life is not yet run.
A long road stretches before me
As I wander towards whatever grand purpose
For which your hands are shaping me.

The wonder, the eagerness
Move me to seek your face,
There perchance to steal a fresh glimpse of who I am in
your eyes
Which see my final form even now,
Which sparkle excitedly as you part the curtains slowly
wider,
Revealing greater blessing than you have already
bestowed.

For what delight compares with holding high a newborn
babe
Entrusted to my care by my own Abba?
What joy transcends seeing you draw near
To loved ones lost in darkest mazes?
What blessing equals giving hope
To those the world has labeled hopeless?
What dance surpasses freedom's dance
When chains no longer bind the feet?

And yet your grace increases,
The glory ever expands,
And strangely I am pleased to say
That with the glory grows the pain,
For pain reveals my weaknesses,
And in them your strength is evident to all,
In them your glory manifest
So as my journey home continues,
Be pleased, Lord, to lead me through dark places,
That your light may shine even brighter
And your love alone sustain me.

Father
(Psalm 68, Psalm 127, Isaiah 49, Matthew 10)

A mistake? An inconvenience?
An impeachment of your blameless facade?
What was it you heard when the news of my conception
Seeped murderously into your tingling ears?

By doing nothing at all
You cut deeper into me than surgeons ever have.
You pierced a soul that had yet no words for pain,
Only a primal wail of worthlessness and hurt.
What else can a heart do when one who should have
leapt for joy
At hearing of a growing life
Instead turned back in fear and shame,
Pronouncing with your deafening silence an enduring
curse
That stole away my worth and value
And left wide open a wound for this hateful world to
poison.

And yet I understand what happened
For I, too, have been blinded by fear,
Have hurt and maimed beloved ones,
Have violated deepest wells of soul's sanctity,
All because I tried to run,
To duck and hide from a waiting cross
Shaped for my own back for my own climb up
surrender's hill

Blaming you does nothing.
It heals no hurts and stops no bleeding,

19

Not in you or in me.
You acted in ignorance,
Not knowing your dart even flew, let alone how true it
would strike.

And God was gracious,
A Father to the fatherless, a lover to the lonely.
He spoke value into my heart.
He leapt for joy at my birth on the shores.
He shone even brighter
When I first saw my name carved into his hands.
How numerous and wondrous his thoughts of me,
How deep and true his love has been.

And would I have known this had you been there?
For God has used your absence to teach me what a Father is,
And what you meant for self-preservation God has used
for good.
Though still sore, the wounds are mending,
And I ask you to forgive me
For holding on so long and silently
To the anguish and hurt your silence birthed,
For cursing you in darkest hours
When the pain throbbed relentlessly, namelessly.
Please forgive me.
I wish you well, father.

Lockdown
(I John 1)

Festering, swelling, infecting the soul,
Rebellion concealed gnaws at my heart.
In chains my tongue groans silently,
Longing for confession, for release,
Hoping a prophet will ask how I really am.
But why should they know? They don't know me.
Help me cry out!
Help my soul find its voice,
For I know you are faithful to cleanse.

Curses
(John 10, Galatians 3)

What is a curse?

A chain you cannot break,
An unending cycle of foolish choices
Harming everyone you love.

Enmeshed in webs we weave ourselves,
We wonder who will set us free,
Whose hand will reach through the putrid mess
And take us out for good.

None but one may work that feat,
He who became a curse himself.
The blood he shed dissolves the strands
Of defensiveness, sin, and pride.
Jesus is this Mighty One
The one who turns each curse into a blessing,
Who transforms terror into glory,
And brings abundant life out of the jaws of death.
He shall make me free.

Zombie Flick
(Romans 6, II Corinthians 10, Ephesians 6)

Black cowl blowing amidst crumbling headstones,
Temptation's dark ritual of rebellion begins again,
Provoking, enticing the dead parts of me
To lumber hungrily like Romero's zombies,
Consuming and destroying all in my path.

But if the horror film can be solved with a shotgun,
How much of a threat can there really be?
And my weapons are fully effective
For tearing down every stronghold still in me.
So I load in shells of prayer and scripture,
Take aim and fire,
One down. Man, that was messy.
Many still to go before the credits roll.

Strange Answers
(Romans 5-6)

I asked you once to lead me through
Places that seldom see the light,
Places angels fear to tread.
I expected battles,
Unbelievers arrayed against me,
Loved ones suffering unspeakably,
Sickness and pain around every bend,
All there to test and refine my hungry heart.
Instead you showed me my naked soul,
Its every longing ferociously corrupt,
Nothing off limits to its bestial impulses,
No temple too sacred to pillage.
In the darkness of those vain imaginations
Every gruesome thought is inescapably mine.
There shame and fear can choke out life
Or mercy and grace release me.

I asked you once to lead me through
Places where your love alone could lead me.
Such a place this is,
Where illusions of my own redeemability
Wither away in the scorching heat of my sin.
Truly hopeless apart from you,
I will walk forward in the light of your mercy,
Beholding whatever measure of my wickedness
You see fit to show me,
And so beholding anew
The unsearchable depths of your relentless love.

Gardening
(Genesis 2, Song of Solomon 4, Ephesians 5, Hebrews 13)

I found new shafts to mine out love
As you packed their bags and yours.
Your brief sojourn with family seldom seen
Awakened in me fond affection I forgot.

Yet, too, it stirred a jealous beast.
Unwilling to share you even so innocently,
My sinful heart would lock you away,
Make you mine exclusively,
Not your own to give your love,
Whether agape, eros, or phileo,
But mine to take whatever love I need,
If love it could be called.
So in your absence I consume elsewhere -
Digital models I can discard with a click,
Unknowing schoolgirls immodestly dressed
Who never see my eyes devour.

Your leaving has revealed my sin:
A longing to control some part of my life,
That secret garden of intimacy.
But even that is beyond my jurisdiction, for I have none.
The earth is the Lord's and everything in it,
Even gardens in my heart.
And why shouldn't they be?
He sows no quickly growing weeds
That blossom early and clutter afterwards,
Fit only to be mowed dejectedly.
He nurtures one slowly blooming fruit-tree

With branches to shade me from noonday heat,
Fruit sweet enough to soothe my soul
And so beautiful I must pick it gently from elegant
branches.

Those weeds I sow cannot compare.
No nourishment lies beneath their sordid skin,
But I impatiently fill my plate with them.
If I would wait for that tree to blossom,
If I would release my expectations
And receive what God would give,
Then perhaps my heart would stop running wild
As I finally learn to rest in trust
That the Lord does in fact love me
And he is in fact the giver of all good gifts,
And you are one of his very best gifts.
This I see by how I yearn for your return.
God knows well what he's doing
In this garden's dry season.
The rains will come upon this fallow ground.
The blossoms will sprout,
And new fragrances will fill our hearts with joy.
I will pull the weeds I've sown
That steal the nourishment you should have from me.
This garden is ours alone;
I will invite no more trespassers
To tread upon this holy ground.

Disappear
(Jonah 1-2, Romans 5, Hebrews 4)

Disappear
Far from here
Flee the fear
No more tears

Truth's incision
Or fading vision
Hard decision
Self-derision

Childish flailing
Heart is ailing
Hear my wailing
Faith is failing

Just let it go
But how do I know
You'll still love me so
Calvary's flow

Absalom
(II Samuel 13-18)

If I cannot see your face
Then it would be better for me to stay far away.
So I tell myself when you feel so far.
In that darkness I sow seeds of mistrust;
Doubt blossoms and bears fruit
As I take control for myself,
Believing the lies I tell myself:
You are unjust,
Uncaring,
Unable.
The need for revolt becomes obvious.
It must be done for the greater good.
I must take what's yours for you can't use it.
What a fool!
My false glory and pride becomes a deadly snare.
Trapped in the wilderness,
Nothing is left for me to do but wait
For you to show me your mercy
Or your sword.

Disconnected
(I Kings 19, Romans 11)

Disconnected,
Hungry for stimulus,
For life to course through my veins.
My flesh always seeks to pull the plug,
To prune me off the vine,
To lead me where I know I can do nothing.
When nothing is what I want to do
The danger is greatest.
Lack of discipline bears its fruit
In hungry eyes and white knuckles.

So now each moment I must choose
Between illicit connection to feed my flesh and quicken
my pulse
Or drawing on the life that flows from you,
The connection that slowly, too slowly
Bears in me a holy fruit,
A righteous fruit,
The fruit of walking step by step with you.

You do not cater to my senses.
You use no pyrotechnics or dazzling stunts
To draw me to yourself.
The flame, the whirlwind, the earthquake,
Though thrilling, hold no trace of you.
Were I to seek you there I would be consumed,
Swept away.
No,
You bid me wait for life,

Wait excruciatingly,
As drop by drop you fill my cup.
You send no flood to quench my thirst,
But only a sufficient draught
To keep me seeking your living water.

So which will I choose?
The immediate, the gratuitous
Or the delayed, the elusive?
This moment I will not choose to settle;
I will choose to seek.

A Fool to His Folly
(Genesis 1, Exodus 32, Psalm 135, Luke 8, Matthew 6, John 11)

The slippery slope of self-willed living
Always leads to the same dark place:
Alone inside the prison of my mind,
No one to feel distant from,
No one to yearn for,
Just myself
Believing I am absolved of all obligation
And rid of all love.
Truly alone is truly in Hell.
We who are made in triune image
Cannot exist in isolation,
Yet I choose it,
The illogical logic of addiction
Making mockery of astounding insights
Into who and why and how I am.
Confounded by the riddle,
Terrified by the uncontrollabe,
I wonder what to do when reason fails.

Yet reason never saved a soul,
Calmed a storm or raised the dead.
The idol of intellect has failed me again.
Blind, deaf, dumb, it does not hear my frightened pleas
Nor see my trembling heart
Or speak a soothing word of love.
It has no hands to rescue me
From nets and snares that block my path,
Yet I ever trust it
Because that idol is me,

And loathe I am to melt that calf.
But melt it must, with all my strongholds,
Bastions of self in a war against me,
Hives of treachery when self-destruction calls.

There is no other God like you
Who grants his servants true freedom.
I have served the others long enough to know
That bondage lies in doing homage at their feet.
The stone and wooden gods I've made have failed me
utterly.
Only you are left to trust,
So give me this day my daily bread,
For tomorrow is more than I can know.
Amen.

Confusion
(Psalm 51, Psalm 139, Isaiah 43, Mark 2)

What would make me doubt your love?
What would turn my heart to stone?
What is it I am in search of
That I can't find before your throne?

Does guilt consume me from within
Or rage at weakness buried deep?
What keeps me running to my sin
Instead of to your solace sweet?

What rebel cries within my soul,
Resisting cleansing sacrifice?
Emotions squirm and twist and roll;
They flee from my inquiring eyes.

But none of this is dark to you.
You search far corners of my heart.
In me you're doing something new,
But first you must break me apart.

Reveal to me the wickedness
That forms the basis for revolt.
Impart to me your holiness,
Though it may burst my wineskins old.

This pain I bring upon myself
Won't make your love from me depart.
Far from thrusting me towards Hell,
You're calling me back to your heart.

Leviticus
(Genesis 22, Leviticus 1-7, Psalm 51, Isaiah 61, Colossians 1, Hebrews 10)

The fire never stopped burning.
Ever the offerings streamed to you -
Oxen, bulls, sheep, pigeons,
All blameless, spotless, innocent,
Laid hold of by priest and layman,
Guilty alike before your holy law,
Slaughtered by hands stainded deeper
Than the blood of sacrifice could ever penetrate.

As the carefully carved flesh was arranged upon your brazen altar
The smoke would rise lazily to your nostrils.
A sweet aroma you called it,
A fragrance pleasing to the Lord.
No doubt you looked ahead to the Lamb you bring -
Perfect, radiant, the one image of you we could dare behold.
He was placed on an altar of love,
Like Isaac before him an only Son,
Like the millions of slaugtered creatures
Slain in place of a wayward son.

So as your people long ago
Laid their hands upon that blameless beast
And so proclaimed the deadly consequence of sin,
I, too, have placed my hand on Christ,
Entrusting even my sin to you,
Releasing it to be consumed by fire

In the consumption of your Son on the cross,
Thus mingling with that sweet aroma the naked trust
Swelling in the hearts that understand it is them
That should be dead and burning on that altar.

That same heart of trust can ravish you
As it daily stands upon your promise of love
No matter how the fire seems to scorch it.
Such a heart waits to be reduced to ashes
For it is only our ashes you will take in exchange for your
beauty.

How long, then, before I confess with all of me
That my castles, my idols, my lusts
Are nothing more than the ashes of shame and sin?
You would gladly take them from me
And for them give me beauty and glory,
Integrity, confidence, faithfulness, focus,
Glaringly lacking in my wandering heart.
You would give me yourself
As the perfume of my admission of bankruptcy
Rises before you with a tearful plea for mercy.

Brokenness and contrition you have never despised.
I am coming to learn these are all I have to offer you.
Accept my gift of slaughtered flesh.
See, I pour the Blood at altar's base,
Knowing that alone has led me to your glory.

Self-Sufficiency
(Psalm 23, Acts 17, Romans 5)

Self-sufficiency—
An illusion of grandest deception,
Clung to with blind tenacity;
A pillar of vain and hopeless living
That cuts me off from sustaining vine.

If I am all I need
Then I surely don't need you,
Or you,
Or you,
And I will never bare my soul,
Or ever live in the freedom of being fully known.
If I am all I need,
My frailty does not need release.
No light need shine in dusty corners of my heart.
If I am all I need
Then I become a slave
To finding answers within that lie without.
I have no strength to lift my heart
Above its own enduring weakness.
I find no love for broken me
If I am all I need.

Self-sufficiency—
An illusion and a cage,
Like any cage.
To disbelieve that lie is to trust that you love me.
To disbelieve is to escape,
To walk through the misty bars,

To break through like mighty waters,
To hear the angels marching in the trees
And claim the victory you already won.

I am not sufficient,
But I am enough.
You love me as I am;
I do not need to wear the mask
Or hide a long corrupted heart.
I am enough as I am,
And your love is more than sufficient
To love past the darkness in my soul
And make me even more than I am.

You wrote my story long ago.
There I will dwell in green pastures
And drink deep of love's still waters,
Abiding in the sufficiency of grace.

Unfulfilled
(I Coritnhians 1, Philippians 3, Hebrews 11, Revelation 14)

The gift of unfulfilled desire
Appears at first anathema.
Why cling to tender promises
That all my days will echo emptily
Across canyons of persistent pain?

Rid myself of that desire
And then I will be rid of pain.
So say many who seem wise.
But you call foolish wisdom's every phoneme
As you call me to embrace that desire—
The unquenchable thirst,
The convulsing longing,
The insatiable hunger
To know you.

I dream small dreams to numb that pain.
If I meet low standards I might forget
Just how deeply I ache for you
And how certain it is that in my flesh I will ever ache.
To flee from that ache is to flee from you,
For you meet me in the center of that pain,
At the fulcrum of the impossibility of knowing you.

The small dreams must shatter.
Counting all things loss, I will embrace emptiness
And in vacuum's agony find you waiting.
I will join those of whom the world is not worthy,
Singing songs of brokenness only I can sing
To Zion's spotless Lamb.

Full of Nothing
(Psalm 1, Mark 9, John 11, John 15, Titus 3, Hebrews 12,)

This ache, this agony erupts from arid emptiness,
Breaking through encrusted flesh devoid of saltiness.
I cannot abide this comfortable withdraw,
This intrusive isolation that invites me ever inward.

Call me out, remove the graveclothes.
Rid me of everything that hinders, all the lovely dross.
You are the light to me eyes,
The breath in my lungs,
The beat of my heart,
The electrifying formation of synapses
In a mind renewed by the washing of water and blood.

Without you I melt like wax,
Wither like every other weed.
In you I flourish, planted by streams of living water,
Tended by hands committed to bringing forth fruit.
In you I am a mighty rock no heat can scorch,
Immovable for its foundation is you, Cornerstone.

Do not let this ache grow numb
Nor the agony lose its edge.
It drives me, chases me into your arms.
Expose the emptiness I crave.
Sweeten the fulness I long to desire.
Satisfy me with thirst for you.

Zeal for Your House
(Job 5, Isaiah 53, John 2:13-25, Romans 6, I Corinthians 6)

Transaction has no place in your house.
So when I come with gold and silver
To buy a sacrifice to offer you,
You pour out my coins and scatter my flocks,
Leaving me with nothing left to offer but myself.

Zeal for your house consumes you,
And you will have nothing defile
The temple of your Holy Spirit.
If you must, scourge you will
For you know that scourging only rends the flesh,
And opens ways for life to burst out
Past the bounds of what the eye may see.
And where you scourge you heal.
Even wounds that lead to death
Only open the door to resurrection.

Let zeal for your house consume me.
Ignite a holy fire that will not abide the flesh
And its vain attempts to earn your grace.
This temple is a house of prayer,
Naked prayer,
Desperate prayer,
Prayer only the ribbons leftover from scourging can
offer,
Broken, waiting for you.

Don't Let Me Go Numb
(I Timothy 4, I John 1)

Don't let me go numb!
Don't let me go numb!
The pain tells me I'm bleeding, rotting,
Shriveling, wasting,
Dying
The pain drives me to you,
Healer of my brokenness,
Mender of my shattered heart,
Torn asunder by my own persistent sin.

Don't let me go numb!
Don't let me go numb!
Don't let me medicate the symptoms
While I allow the cancer to swallow my soul.
Don't let me linger in darkness,
Unable to see the harm I cause.
Shine your light! Reveal the wounds.
Though I inflicted them I must face them.
Though they are the work of my guilty hands
I must behold them with my guilty eyes.

Don't let me go numb!
Don't let me go numb!
That icy chill consumes all warmth,
Removing all desire to forge connection,
To tear down walls of isolation,
Dulling my senses as I forget how valuable I am.

Don't let me go numb!
Don't let me go numb!

The grueling work of intimacy
Requires a depth of feeling known infrequently
In the desert of emotional anorexia,
But how needed is that depth
As islands grow tiresome
And peace and quiet become an earsplitting hush.

Feeling never meant as much as now;
Intimacy never wore a more alluring garment;
Embracing your image was never more enchanting
Than in these days of building bridges
Across the ocean of my insecurity and fear
Into your glorious light.

Perseverance of the Saints
(Psalm 26, Jonah 2, Matthew 14, Acts 27, Galatians 6)

Persevering until the end
Seems unattainable at times.
Waves of sin and doubt and fear
Ever shatter the vessel of my faith.
Yet there you stand atop the tide
Of everything I fear might keep me from you.
Lord, if it's you, then bid me walk,
Transfix these wandering eyes with your beauty
That I might not turn away and sink,
My life's breath failing as I slip away.

Still, those shipwrecked you preserved.
Those cast overboard you raised up again.
Surely no storm, no beast, nothing created can separate me.
All that's left are my own sinful choices.

I cannot see this tent's last days,
So to boast of where my heart will be
When sulllied flesh resolves to dew
Is folly unabashed.
Only moment by moment can I be sure.
Thus you say, "Examine yourself."
I know your law; by that I judge.
My tomorrows I commit to you;
I will love you today.

Visibility
(Job 3, II Corinthians 5)

Why is light given to him who suffers?
Would not the darkness be a better friend?
Sight and vision bring only gruesome reminders of pain.
But is it not when torment parts the clouds of comfort
That we see most clearly?
Does not a dousing in ice-cold anguish
Wake us from the slumber of prosperity?
God's face shines brightest when Sheol bears its fangs,
And in that darkness we behold love.

Why is light given to those whose way is hidden,
Whom God has hedged in?
Is not seeing the shame of waywardness a cruel taunt?
Surely death would be more welcome
Than listlessly staring at obstructing mountains.
Yet is not life itself found in these blind seasons?
For the righteous shall live by faith,
And there is no faith when eyes can be trusted.
When light is given to the lost,
They do not see their path
But rather salvation's strong arm.

Light comes to those in pain, those lost,
To reveal God's face
When vision is best.

Planted
(Psalm 1, John 4, John 15, Romans 11)

Reaching desperately for the beams of sunlight,
Searching long and far for water under every rock and
stone,
Planted in an arid spot to feed a dying people with my
fruit.
I cannot do this on my own.
Without you my fruit is poison.
Without you my roots disappear, withered by the heat.
Prune me.
Strip away everything that chokes the water,
Every unfruitful part of me.
Tear up the weeds my old seed became.
Burn up the thorns, the vines that strangle and smother.
Let your water flow through every vein.
Turn me to your light.
Draw me into it and flourish me,
A tree at home in Eden.

Inspiration
(Psalm 84, Isaiah 53, Zephaniah 3, John 1, Romans 8,
II Corinthians 12)

What's behind the music?
What inspires the song?
What fuel makes the artist tick
And drives the muse along?

In me a well of untapped pain,
Strangely cool to silent throat.
That waiting draught I would disdain
But for your promise, though remote.

I fear to pass through darkened door;
The looming tears and shame do mock.
They say I'm worthless to the core,
Too small to stand upon the Rock.

I nod with them in blind consent,
Isolating for my sin.
With misery I grow content,
That treacherous, enabling friend.

You sing a different song to me.
Your blood-stained hands enfold my heart.
Inviting me upon your knee,
You teach me how to live my art.

Through darkened door my freedom lies.
In that well is truth's sweet wine.
There the God my pen describes
Becomes true Abba, Father of mine.

There weakness causes celebration
And frailty wears the greatest crown.
From broken hearts spring adulation
For him who from the heavens came down.

Grief's companion, sorrowful,
He walked upon our loveless sod.
In meekness he was powerful,
The Living Word, the flesh-wrapped God

He bids me walk down dreary road
With him to guard me from the night.
Though shame and fear and doubt forbode
I will abide in love's warm light.

Embracing pain sets loose the bard.
My weakness does God's strength reveal.
No heartache will my pen retard,
Nor any trial my hope conceal.

Significance
(Matthew 6, John 12, Romans 2)

Vital organs, 20k
You say let go, I must obey.
For these I seek the praise of men,
Trying to steal your glory again

Worst of all you say lay down
Ever knowing I'm renown.
Significance defined by me
Denies who you want me to be.

Such is Faith

*(Genesis 22, Genesis 39, Psalm 23, Psalm 31, Song of Solomon
5, Isaiah 9, Hebrews 12, Revelation 10)*

This soul's dark night my love grows cold.
The dizzying heights of holy vision
Seem far from my fleshly eyes.
The mystery of knowing my Lord
Seems old and gray, a forgotten dream.
Prayers are empty and hollow; the altar's flame has
dimmed.

What will keep me seeking you
When the sensation and emotion
Have evaporated in the heat of earthly desert?
Only love, resilient and stubborn,
Tenacious obedience, no matter the agony,
No matter the absence of anything at all.
To apprehend you by faith is to apprehend
When no grip is felt,
When your weight is the that of air,
Present in its absence.
You do not lend yourself to easy love,
Without obstacles and barriers
To be overcome when all within us screams, "Rebel!"
Such is faith, to believe with no basis save your word.
Neither heart nor mind feel compelled,
Only a spirit crying out for you,
Yearning for you,
More desperate for you than words could ever convey.
For what man knows the depth of his own need,
The scope of his own barrenness?

Our blindness would leave us creeping to our destruction,
Some slowly, some quickly.
But we who dwell in darkness have seen a great light,
Awakening from a sleeping dream that we have tried so hard to quell.

To heed it is to lay down and die,
Or rather admit we're already dead.
And in this season I find this intolerable.
Sin writhes deep within my soul.
Selfishness simmers like some witch's brew,
Belching forth foul curses and hellish torment.
This cup you've given me is bitter to my senses.
Far better to have John's scroll,
Honey going down that turned the stomach in the end.
For I am living shortsightedly,
Eager and willing for pleasures that come quickly and easily,
Heedless of the violent convulsions of sorrow I know they bring.
I know when I imbibe your draught,
Though scalding and nauseous it now seems,
It will sweeten and fill my heart with joy,
For to drink is to die to myself
And walk in blessing I could never guess.

So in this darkness of my soul
With no lamp to show me where my foot may fall,
You offer me this hemlock to my flesh.
Such is faith.
Moriah could not slay the promise,

Potiphar's chains kept nothing prisoner,
And the cross held only glory for the suffering servant.
So what fear swirls in goblet's depths?
That life will no longer bend to my wishes,
As if it ever did.
That time will no longer be my servant,
As if it ever was.
That I might no longer chart my on course,
As if I ever could.
Only colossal folly paralyzes me,
Abject arrogance alone hinders me.

What hope is there for a stubborn fool such as I?
Dare I imagine mustering sufficient will to defeat my will?
Within my bones resides no strength to ingest this envenomed cure.
Lame, I lie leprous, self-abused and robbed.
Hold the cup to my lips, I'll swallow.
I'll pass again through death to life.
There can be no waking without sleep,
No healing without sickness,
No resurrection without death.
I choose this death that I might live your life,
That I might find you in the secret place
And dwell in your house forever my Lord and King.
Amen.

Plain White Tee
(Psalm 139)

When you wear a plain white tee
You are innocuous.
No one sees you as shallow
And over concerned with fashion;
It's just a plain white tee.
No one sees a derelict;
It's just a plain white tee.

When you wear a plain white tee
The storms pause for just a moment,
Just long enough for you to catch your breath.
It's just a plain white tee;
What seething and boiling
Could possibly be underneath?

Feasting on Locusts
(Joel 2, Matthew 3)

What is this darkening the midday sky?
What's this clatter disturbing afternoon respite?
The escalating cacophony foreshadows destruction.
The advancing blackness reveals the barrenness about to
consume me
As you send out your great army:
The creeping locust,
The swarming locust,
Every locust that will devour
The fruit of every seed I have sown,
The weeds that choke away true life
Along with those fruits which seem so rich,
So right and good.

You will strip me bare,
Painfully released from all I thought I needed,
For in your removing you are giving,
As you did that voice in Judah's waste,
Locusts upon which to feast.

Healing
(*John 4:46-5:17*)

Is it a sign I am after
Because my faith is so small?
Or is my prayer a simple one,
An honest need from an honest heart
As my son lays dying?

You want me to ask the question
But you already know the answer,
And it doesn't matter to you
For you love regardless
And feel my pain as your own.
So stretch out your hand
Or even just your voice
Or just will it,
For you are the King of Glory
And all creation bows before your throne.
Whether the 7th hour or the 11th
I know your love will deliver.

Now ask a different question,
For here I am a 38 year cripple
With no one to help me to the healing pool.
Do I want to be healed?
Of course.
38 years with healing right in front of me
And yet still lame
Should not suggest I am comfortable.
My pallet has not molded perfectly to my frame,
Nor do life's responsibility frighten me.

Do I want to get well?
Now that you ask, no.

But you see a future for me
That surpasses my greatest dreams,
So I let go of my excuses
And respond to your great vision.

So which am I in truth?
The desperate man with burning needs:
Fulfillment, purpose, purity,
Or the comfortable one,
Pleased with brokenness you could heal?
Both depending on the second.
The good news for me is that you loved both men.
You met them in their world, their hurt.
So you will meet me whereever I find myself,
And you will bring the right healing
The right way at the right time,
For you do all things well, Gracious King.

Unwilling
(Matthew 6, Luke 10)

I think I must have misheard you.
You who love me completely would never have asked
for that.
Surely I am hearing things,
For you desire my good, my joy, my prosperity.
So I will stop my ears and sing your praises.
I will shout your greatness and loudly live your glory
Because I know your voice, and you would never say
that,
Would you?
And I wouldn't want to stop to listen
To voices I know can't be yours.

So let the clatter of praise continue,
Drowning out every hint of relationship.
Pious blatherings shelter me
From hearing you speak discomfort and growth.
Who has time for that, anyway,
With all we have to do to prepare for your arrival?

The Beauty of Redemption

Blessed Emptiness
(Deuteronomy 4, Luke 12, John 12, II Timothy 4, Revelation 2)

Blessed emptiness fill my soul.
Rich poverty be my kingly crown.
Shatter me to make me whole.
Build me up through tearing down.

Pour me out like sweet perfume,
Washing feet that tread through sin.
May holy fragrance fill the room
When through my deeds you enter in.

Let me no more build bigger barns
To store my temporal rewards.
Before I wake those dreams are gone,
So I must cut impeding cords.

Please take my heart and wring it clean,
Removing this world's final drop,
Then soak me in the spirit's stream
And with me wash the coming crop.

Consuming fire purify
Till naught but you gaze from the flames.
Let all that stinks of flesh now die.
I long to hear, Lord, my new name.

Araunah's Threshing Floor
(Exodus 16, IISamuel 24, Romans 6)

I will not offer painless praise
Or walk the broad and gentle path.
Blessings hoarded mold like mana,
Breeding maggots that anesthetically devour
All hope of caring for more than me.
The gospel of bloody restoration,
Of healing through the cross of anguish
Knows no such bargain sacrifice.
My gift to God shall cost me dearly,
Not for my own baptized boastfulness,
But because in letting go of me and mine
I find room in my heart I never knew I had
For gathering in the hurting and hungry,
For sheltering the homeless far from home,
Whose lives and loves a shackled world has washed
away.

In the Trenches
(Romans 6)

Entrenched to stay, pinned down by choice,
Though pierced, bleeding, and maimed
My heart bids me stay
Because you stayed unto death.

What still baffles me, though,
Is the mission you've assigned.
I am to die in this war
And walk away victorious in you.
For the war is in me
And over me
And against me.

The enemy, oft dormant, strikes silently,
Coming with stealth, assaulting rapidly,
But I cannot simply defend.
You call me to attack,
To charge heedlessly up the Hill
To reclaim land in my soul
Long underneath the tyranny of sin.

Slain in battle, you raise me up
And seat me at the victor's feast.
There with all those the grave could not hold
We'll celebrate the life hidden in death.

Spoils of War
(Jeremiah 51, Lamentations 3, Romans 6, I Peter 2, I John 2)

The dust departs the battlefield.
The earth is scorched within my soul.
The enemy at last did yield
But how this fight has taken toll.

Weak and wounded arms fall limp,
No strength left to hold this sword.
Lift me up and help me grip
The spoils from this war.

First fear's absence—drink it deep.
The furtive backwards glances fade.
A pure heart next for me to keep,
My darkness now replaced with day.

No more shame from selfish acts,
The battle's Blood has scoured me.
I stand up tall without a mask.
From bondage you have set me free.

My loved ones find me fresh and new.
Beyond myself I learn to look.
Fear to freedom I've passed through,
Reclaiming what the enemy took.

The ruthless slaughter of our flesh
Leaves none but you to hail as Lord.
Your Spirit arises, gives new breath.
In truth, you are the spoils of war.

Psalm 24.1
(Genesis 3, Psalm 24)

Shut away by ancient doors,
Doors of sin and shame as old as one rebllious bite.
Trapped behind imposing gates,
Gates of fear and selfishness
Steadfastly barring my escape.

Lift up your heads, O gates,
And be lifted up you ancient doors;
Let the King of Glory come in.
He is a mighty warrior,
Mighty in battle and able to deliver me
From sin's every creeping tendril.

The Lord of Hosts will rescue me;
My God will rejoice over me.
The ancient doors, my prized idols,
Will be no more,
And I will ascend the hill of the Lord,
Hands and heart cleansed by your blood,
Dew that brings mysterious strength,
New each morning, enough for each day.

No more will I lift my soul to another.
I will seek the face of the God of Jacob,
For the earth and all who dwell therein,
And thus my heart,
Are his beloved possession.

Graffitti
(Phillippians 2)

"I love you with all my heart,"
Said the graffitti on the 295 overpass
Headed east on Church Road.
"Who loves who?" I wondered idly.
Clearly desperation fueled this fire.
Perhaps someone trying to make amends
Or maybe inviting them to be made.
Someone took his life in his hands
To post this love note in view of all.
Dangerous,
Risky,
Like any real love, I suppose.

Then I understood that message.
I had read it many times before,
Only now to see it clearly.
As far as I will ever know
The love note was for me.
You who went to greatest lengths,
Forsaking glory, throne, and life,
To say in sweetest tones
That you love me with all your heart,
Stretched out your hand again
Just to remind me of your love
In case I had forgotten.

Gentle
(Exodus 32, Psalm 16, Matthew 6)

Ssshhh. Be still.
Your restless heart ever pounds in my ear
As your frenetic search for meaning and fulness
Cracks its whip upon your shredded back.

Why are you still searching?
You've found yourself inside my love.
Your worth's defined by my shed blood.
Are you still so vain that you try to find your pleasure far
from me?
Be sure your sin is not in your deeds,
But in your wayward, wandering heart
That turns the good things I have given
Because of my great love for you
Into idols I must always grind to dust and mix with your
drink
That you might remember the bitterness in not seeking
me.

Silence now. Hear the Spirit.
Do not heap guilt upon your head;
This wandering was paid for long ago.
Only return from your futile journeys.
You know my embrace is your home,
You know fulness of joy is in my hand,
So stay forever under my wings.
Seek me first and let me add the rest.

Dare I Believe It
(I Samuel 5, Psalm 23, Ephesians 3)

Dare I believe it,
That you will provide for me out of your riches in glory?
That you are wholly sufficient to fill the longings of my
heart?
Dare I embrace the upheaval that would bring
As idols, beloved but lifeless, tumble down,
Dismembered as Dagon by your righteous sword?
Will I walk through the darkness of trusting you
completely,
Relinquishing my vain and foolish thirst for control?

Death's shadow looms ominously over earthly vale,
But a shadow is all it is.
In such a dreadful night as this
I can only whisper as a child,
"You love me,
You love me,"
Again and again, over and over,
Till doubting flesh gives way to a heart of trust
And eyes fixed by fear on selfishness
Turn expectantly in hope to you,
Giver of all good gifts,
Abba,
Father.

Canaan
(Numbers 13, Joshua 6, Psalm 27)

There are surely giants in the land,
Menacing me with insurmountable size.
When I dare look at myself
I see how small I really am.

"Forward, Love," you say to me,
Standing glorious amidst the fray.
"No."
My answer comes flatly, lamely.
The battles are too many, too fierce,
Too taxing on a wretch like me.
I want passivity which I mistake for peace.
I want nothing more than my family fed and my leisure
mine,
But your call is higher,
Higher than I can fathom,
So stratopheric that vertigo sets in
When I but steal a glimpse of my heart's Canaan.

There the milk and honey flow
Only when I am willing to stand before the giants,
To confront them by name:
In me, Defensiveness and Judgmentalism,
Foul twins that build great walls,
Cutting off the ones I love.
Their sires, Fear and Rejection,
Keep them well fed, well trained.
How do I battle such fearsome foes,
Tiny grasshopper that I am?

I don't, I can't,
But you, Great Father, Adonai
Have removed their protection—the deepest darkness in
my soul.
Your light goes forth, exposing their weakness.
All that's left for me to do is arrive in faith,
And you will drive them out before me.

Such trust is dangerous.
"What if there is failure?" I ask in the dark hours.
What would that mean I am?
Unloveable, hopeless.
Is that an option, though?
Arriving in faith and facing defeat
Means you have failed, not I.
Once again my fears prove absurd.
Your goodness and your love dispel them
As the late spring breeze dispels oppressive heat.
One choice is left for me to make -
To trust you for the moment's battle,
Not tomorrow's or next year's.
Canaan did not fall in a single rout
Nor even Jericho in one day.
So my heart will not be purified in a single sleepless night
Of fervent prayer and fasting.
The battle, though won by you,
Will still extract from me anguished tears and lonely cries,
But never more than I can bear,
For your ardent love will keep me, seal me.
You'll spread your tabernacle over me
And quench my thirst.

"Forward, Love," you say again,
A flame of passion in your eyes.
"Yes, Lord," comes my answer unexpectedly.
Your love has blazed a trail,
Though winding it may be.
I will enter that fabled land,
I will taste the milk and honey,
One step, one drop at a time.

Worship
(Psalm 139, Song of Solomon 2, Revelation 4)

Worship is me,
Defenseless, powerless,
Without pretense or facade,
Presented to you just as I am,
For that is how you crafted me.
To present my self to you as I wish I were
Is to deny your power
And my weakness
And spin a lie that blows away like leaves
In the gale of your ever-searching spirit.

As surely as I want to hide,
Even more do you wish to find me
And pour your love out on who I truly am.
The illusions, the mirages, the many masks
Cannot receive your boundless grace;
You did not make them.
They cannot come with incense to your glorious throne;
You did not purchase them.
It was not for them you bled and died,
It was for the last person I want to be—
Me,
Naked before you,
Unveiled before you,
Or rather before myself,
For no disguise conceals me from the Seven-fold Spirit
Nor any fortress I build withstand your seven great
horns.
As you ever pursue me.

By that most intimate pursuit
You persuade me of the safety of worship,
Coaxing me gently down from my cleft in the rocks,
Making me unaware of my own nakedness.
I am too taken with your beauty,
Concerned only with bringing you true worship.
In that place my guard is let down,
My walls melt away,
And by your goodness I learn to trust you with my heart.

Drummer Boys
(Matthew 5, Luke 2, Luke 21)

The poor in spirit play their drums by your cradle—
A humble gift for a humble king.
The steady thumping of their offering,
The rhythmic sacrifice of praise
Is richer than the finest present
The wealth of fallen men could buy.

So as two kingly coppers clinked,
Magnificently released from a widow's lonely hand.
So, too, every beat and thump,
Every resonating pulse
Resounds through your manger.
There the lowly Lord in swaddling bands
Sets the pace for every drummer
Longing to play in time with God.

Loves Much
(Luke 7:36-50)

The dirt and grime of byways soils your feet,
Yet no basin or towel or servant
Was offered to extend the basic hospitality of cleaning.

The dirt and grime of darker byways
Where I have given myself away to wolves
Soils my lonely soul,
And no basin have I found
Or towel or servant who would stoop to wash
A sinner such as I.

No one until I heard you speak of forgiveness,
Of Father God who loves his children.
At once I knew I had a home in you.

When I heard you'd come to Simon's house,
I had to see you, to hear your voice,
And there you were, neglected, dirty,
Unwelcome for the dirt you bore.

Father God, who loves his children,
Would wash those feet with tender care.
Unthinking, I raced in, poor as ever.
No towel or basin to offer you,
But just a love of gratitude
Poured out from within a fragile vessel.
You have need Lord. I will go
And, with water from a living well within,
I'll wash your feet so soon to bleed.

My hair, once used to lure and trap,
I'll now adorn with holy filth,
For even that is richer than the gold of kings.

I'll bear your grime sweet Lord, each speck,
For you have borne each speck of mine.

Being a Son
(Genesis 1, Mark 1, Romans 8)

My Daddy made the moon for me,
To light the night, to light my face.
He loves to see me smile.
We played catch with the stars before he scattered them
across the sky.
We'll go fishing tonight, too,
And draw many out of darkness.
Time with Daddy in the night
Makes the dawn a sweeter gift.
The rippling shadows now concealing
Will be dispelled,
And I will see him smiling back.

Heartbeat
(I Corinthians 2)

Your heartbeat's my compass and your word's my map
As I'm lost in the wilderness of knowing you.
Purest brooks of renewing mercy
Hem me in and guard my ways.
Trees of faithfulness tower before me,
Simple and deep in their timelessness.

Alone in this sweet communion
Where the dew serves as wine and the earth your bread
Your heartbeat is clearer and louder.
Lord let it draw me and break me
And lose me in the overgrowth of abundant life.
Bring me over the streams, closer and deeper.
Haunt me, lure me with ancient rhythm
Till the subsonic throb of divine love
Embraces me tightly in your bosom.
There I will listen to your heartbeat forever.

Mountain Climbing
(Psalm 16, Psalm 84, Phillippians 3)

Many mountains mark the way,
Each a challenge fit for growth.
Yet many people never get on past the first.
They plant their flags upon their molehills
And place a burger crown upon their brows,
Proclaiming lustily, "I've arrived!"
Looking back they feel so tall.

If only they would turn around
They'd see the next peak beckoning.
From there the next comes into view,
And then the next,
And then the next.
For each is but a foothill
On the steep climb to God's heart.
That mountain we will climb forever,
Drinking in the grandeur of each step,
Knowing thirst and quenching shall ever flow from his
eyes.

The Beauty of Purpose

Deity's Dream
(Romans 8, Ephesians 2)

Does God dream?
Does he yearn for the future he's written
To unfold before our eyes?
Or is he already there,
Brilliant in his glory,
Seated on his throne of grace and justice?

Does he quiver in anticipation,
Waiting to move his hand of power?
Or does his omniscience,
His eternity through time
Allow him to walk demurely through the miracles?

Does God dream,
Dream of what I might become
If I would finally grow up?
Or does knowing the end from the beginning
Squelch the mystery and grow the peace?

Surely I ask because I dream,
But is dreaming part of his imprinted image?
Or, darker, quiet rebellion in my heart,
Discontent with what he's given, what he's done?

But then
Is there even a difference
Between prophets and dreamers?
Perhaps just the heart that births the vision.

One thing I know:
If God does dream
I will share that dream
Sleeping soundly in Abba's hands.

Valley of the Shadow
(Luke 8, II Corinthians 3)

Shadows flicker all around me,
Not so fearsome as one might think,
Comfortable, even, though not as shade,
For I am one with them.
Shifting, ceasing, ever concealing,
And yet suggesting some greater form,
Something not yet seen by those like me,
Who walk still in shaded vale.

Light approaches unceasingly,
Preparing to banish this maze of darkness,
To reveal as nothing our grandest boasts,
Our bravest deeds and cruelest works.
Every shadow will melt away,
Even the shadow of me,
Which is all I ever thought I knew.

What will that Light reveal?
A form, a truth, a reality,
Familiar, alien all at once,
No longer a rippling reflection
Or a faded photo,
No more crude models and empty husks,
Something perceived but never seen,
Something I can only trust will be,
For my shadowed eyes have not the strength
To look upon what I will be,
Or am,
Or truly am.
Which, I cannot say.

I know the shadow shortens, though,
And whatever is to be of me creeps slowly into view,
A glimpse here, a tease there,
Whetting a holy hunger
For something I have never before tasted
But which will satisfy me finally to the core.

Drafting the Dead
(Genesis 3, Psalm 18, Job 17, Psalm 144, Ezekiel 37, John 11,
Romans 12, Ephesians 6, Hebrews 10)

A warrior's cry, a trumpet's call
Beckons you, summons you, one and all.
Arise dry heap of dust and bones!
Living host, heed martial tones!

For ages you have slumbered here,
Trapped by sin and doubt and fear.
Your King calls, "Lazarus, come forth!
Take up again your shield and sword!"

You mighty men of Sovereign King,
Your hearts to brazen altar bring.
He'll clean and train your hands for war.
Rise up and fight for your reward.

Your arrogance in garden sweet
Robbed you, left you incomplete.
But by Christ's blood you've been redeemed.
Now live your faith; no more just dream.

3:20
(Joshua 6, Judges 7, I Samuel 5, Isaiah 40, Ezekiel 37, Luke 10,
John 3, Ephesians 3, I Corinthians 1)

How big dare I dream?
Can I envision this heap of dry bones around me
Joined again, wrapped in flesh,
Living, breathing, praising you?

Is there hope within
That all the lies I've told myself
Of uselessness and mediocrity
Will finally, fully melt away
As obscuring mist flees before the dawn's rays?

Do I believe you have great plans for me,
Plans beyond conglomerous anonymity?
Am I finally willing to take responsibility,
Willing to praise down walls
And scatter great hosts with lamps and trumpets?

Come and do the unthinkable, Lord.
Increase as I decrease,
Shame this world's wisdom with me, your fool.
Make a highway in the mountains,
Cut the head and hands off every idol
Till you alone are magnified
By each pulse of my heart,
By each breath counting down my departure home.
You love me for myself,
Not my contribution to your body,
And you will do amazing things

Through a unkempt, near-sighted beggar,
By which you alone will get the glory
While I sit at your feet
In reverent awe at all your hands have wrought.
This I dare dream.

Ambition

(Genesis 17, Genesis 25, II Samuel 16, I Chronicles 11, Psalm 45, II Corinthians 3, Philippians 3, Hebrews 12, James 1)

You speak to me a mirror.
There I see but dimly
Each glorious step of change.
I will not forget these visions.
Ever before my inner eye will I keep them,
For I see that beyond all my companions
You have anointed me with the oil of joy.
I will keep the vision and be blessed.
I will possess all that you have given me:
From Sinai to Euphrates
Each grain of sand upon which I tread.

I will raise up princes, warriors,
Mighty men who fetch living water
Stored behind garrisons of Phillistines.
I will raise up queens,
Daughters of kings who will reign in purity,
All this by your hand upon me.

I will look into the perfect law of liberty
And never, ever forget.
Finding freedom in what shall soon come to pass,
I leave what is behind
That I may lay hold of what you have set before me.
No bowl of porridge shall lure me away from my
birthright.
Nor any stone thrower cause me to speak ill of what you
shall make me.

Eyes opened, ears unstopped,
The lame dancing before your throne—
I want nothing less from your hand.

Moving On
(Numbers 9, John 14, Ephesians 2)

Your works in me declare you praise
Holy, awesome in every way.
Yet greater still the work you'll do
As time brings us closer, Lord, to you.

Were we to marvel at the past,
To camp around what you did last,
No matter how your glory shined
Our faith would fail; we'd miss your mind.

Our hands are set upon the plow.
We look not back but praise you now.
We shall see greater things than those.
Towards Zion's fullness we will go.

Best Man
(John 3:22-36)

With each honor I relinquish,
With each accolade released,
I am privileged to diminish,
I am blessed to know decrease.

This moment it was never mine
But yours, resplendent King,
To sun and moon and stars outshine
While your glories each voice sings.

I've pointed all I could to you.
No glory did I seek.
My joy is the best man's due,
To see you and your bride complete.

So come from Heaven Son of God.
Testify of truth and love.
Disperse your Spirit far abroad
To those who've hidden hope above.

I'll fade into obscurity
For glory goes to you alone.
I'll bask in anonymity
And cast my crowns before your throne.

Come and See
(John 4:1-29, 39-45)

How is it that you speak to me,
So far removed from what you are.
What do you thirst for that I could give?
What dryness could parch you so severely
That you ask someone like me for water?

I know my sin well,
A thousand promises broken.
Ten thousand lies have passed my lips,
And you would make living water well up within me
That I may never thirst again?

Uncomfortable, I try to distract you
With questions that show my erudition.
You cut them out from under me
With Spirit and Truth,
Leaving me but one recourse,
Worship.

No more will this well water satisfy;
It's kept me thirsty all my life.
No more will this waterpot weigh me down.
"Come and see," I'll tell them all.
"Come and see a man who knows my need
And meets it abundantly.
Come and see Messiah King.
Leave the water pots you've used to draw up vanity
And draw from him, the Spring of Life.
Come and see."

Bread
(Matthew 4, Luke 15, John 4:31-38)

Man does not live by bread alone,
Nor even by hearing your word,
But doing it is a sumptuous meal,
A gourmet feast nourishing deep within.
Doing your word is sowing and reaping
Both in my heart and the hearts of others.
And what bounty shall be harvested
By clean and faithful hands!

At that harvest feast the Wine flows freely.
The fattened calf is slaughtered
As the lost are welcomed home.
At that feast servants abound
For the fruit of love has burst forth in each heart.

Send me to the fields, Lord,
I'll not watch them any longer.
Send me, sickle in hand,
For I desire to harvest those whitened heads.
My heart, the world, the fields are one.
Lord of the Harvest, let me serve.

Fish and Loaves
(Mark 2:22, John 6:1-14)

The crowd is hungry
And food is a long journey off,
For this is a remote place.
"Feed them," you say.
I have no fortune to buy enough bread.
I have no storehouse from which to supply them.
Just five barley loaves and two fish,

A poor meal for a poor boy.
"Feed them," you say again.
Reluctant, confused, I surrender my meal.
You bless it.
You thank the Father for the provision
And my generosity,
And the many are fed by your hand,
Not just kept from starving,
But filled,
Completely satisfied by what you provide.
And just to twist the knife of grace,
There was more left over than what I gave you.

Indeed I am poor,
With little, precious little,
To offer the hungry world,
So many in remote places far from your light.
Take my fish and my loaves.
Alone they will do nothing,
But you bless them

And that is sufficient.
Though I empty myself
You will fill me with new wine,
Stretching me to hold even more.

Pregnant
(Genesis 22, Genesis 31, ISamuel 1, Romans 8,
Galatians 3, Titus 3)

Pregnant,
Ready to deliver at last.
Twins, triplets, n-tuplets,
Or a single rosy-cheeked newborn,
Whatever;
I just want it out.

Conceived before there was even a world to be formless
and void,
You planted them in the womb of my heart,
There for me to nurture as I may,
Though that process is still a mystery.

So hear now your bride,
Too long living in barrenness.
Compared to Sarah, still a spring chicken
So I know you are able.
Bring the contractions of labor.
By that miracle of new birth,
Wash those precious infants in your word.
Clothe them in righteousness.
Clothe them in Christ.

Hear me as you heard Rebekah,
Though I too have hidden idols.
Hear me as you heard Hannah,
For I know I have ever been your beloved
Though I have given you no children.

Hear me as you hear creation,
Longing for the release of your sons.
Let the birth pangs come
That I may be barren no longer.

Cocktail
(John 1, Esther 5)

5 parts passion, longing;
4 parts fear, inadequacy —
A powerful emotional cocktail
Sending white hot fire through my veins,
Stripping away all notions of propriety,
Leaving me exposed and raw,
Eager to see you move your hand,
Terrified to stand up and be your tool.

Humiliation waits if you renege,
If you remain merely in the realm of knowledge and
poetry.
But if you cross into experience,
If you live up to being the Living Word
Then I am responsible, accountable.
I cannot remain a spectator to redemption's drama,
Drowsing in the theatre's comfortable seats.

The stage you prepared for me awaits;
The spots are on,
No make-up or costumes to disguise me.
Transparency is the only garb that will do,
Heart-felt improvisation the only acceptable script.

Cut the rope, pull the plug.
Leaping joyfully into the lightless void
Is what I choose.
Please catch me.

Temple Building

(I Chronicles 17, I Chronicles 23, I Chronicles 28,
II Chronicles 1, II Chronicles 6)

Man of war, my house you shall not build.
Your hands besmirched with giant's blood
Will never find their skill in glory and beauty.
The man of peace who follows you —
His hands are clean, his heart is wise.
He will found my house on gold and precious jewels.

You have laid up ore and wood,
The wealth and spoil of your many wars.
He will take your dream, your vision,
And with skill and competence give it frame and flesh.
The house for me birthed in your heart,
Seen only there by trusted eyes,
Will shine a beacon and a standard
Upon land you have died to reclaim.

My people shall turn their faces towards it,
Seeking healing and deliverance.
From there my help shall come to them.
They will know I am the Lord,
Enthroned between the cherubim,
Manifested in my house the man of peace shall build.
Well done.

Adullam
(Genesis 3, I Samuel 22, Psalm 97, Psalm 144, I Corinthians 15, II Corinthians 10, I Peter 1, Revelation 12)

The burden of vision thrusts me down.
The weight of distance between what lies before my eyes
And what waits at the end of faith's long road,
That weight immobilizes,
Intimidates with hopeless words,
Indoctrinates with serpent's counsel.
Is it really your plan?
Is it truly the very rhythm of your yearning heart
To use me,
To make me a builder of houses and armies
Dedicated, consecrated to you, Mighty King?
Did you really say to quarry stones
To shape them for their place in a holy temple?
The very words I hear you speak
I now confuse with voiceless wind
As the dragon spews his river of vanity and doubt
To wash away my trust
Slowly, as a river carves its canyon in the mightiest rock.

Take courage, my soul, for you are no weakling.
Your hands have been trained for war,
Your fingers for battle
By Adonai, the Mighty One,
Who armed the cherubim with swords of aflame,
Who smote nations fat with man's strength,
Whose caress makes mountains tremble,
Whose wrath shall turn the earth to dust,
Whose cross sundered sin's power

And pulverized the stone-cold hands of death.
My weapons are fully effective for tearing down these strongholds,
My armor for for defeating fell dragon's blows.
My hands are trained for war,
Yet tender with a craftman's touch.
So you have created me, called me,
And so I shall be, for your word does not fail.

The burden of vision, disequilibrium's weight
Shall not bend my back as Egypt's chains once did,
But rather teach me kingship as I wait in Adullam for my throne.
Let Saul pursue this anointing.
He shall only prove the character you've built in me,
And I will build it in return
Into those you bring to my quarry.

Builder, Warrior, King, Priest.
So you are,
So must I be.

Storm Clouds
(Song of Solomon 3, Isaiah 24, Isaiah 49, Haggai 2, Ephesians 5, I Peter 2, Revelation 19)

Billowing, mustering on the horizon,
Dark clouds foretell a coming storm.
All I have built will surely shake.
Beams and boards will scream in anguish
As the wind tests their workmanship.

But this house will stand.
Founded on the Chief Cornerstone,
No storm shall move me,
Only prove me,
Only reveal and strip away what's not of you.

You have begun a good and mighty work.
This storm will stir up shouts of praise,
For the coming rain means harvest,
Lives changed, hearts transformed,
New adornments for the bride who makes herself ready.
Here her cry out, "Come,
Out of the wilderness my Beloved comes,
The smoke from his fiery glory a sweet perfume
Announcing his long awaited arrival.
His reward is with him."

This storm will shake kingdoms and thrones.
Strongholds will tumble,
Captives will go free, sleepers awake
All in Jesus name.
They shall say in the ears of those once barren and bereft,

"We need more space; this home is too small."
Raise the valleys and level the great peaks.
Nothing shall hinder those you call home.
Your arm is not too short nor your strength lacking.
You shall rescue the prisoner, relieve the burdened
For your sake and the glory of your name.
Amen.

Two Keys
(Psalm 103, II Corinthians 5)

Two keys kept safely around your neck,
A dangling reminder to me
That you alone unlock my future,
You alone open wide the door of destiny
Through which my purpose is found.
My heart is enlarged,
My potential realized.

That hopeful key jingles against another,
For you also hold the key to my past,
And that door you have shut tightly.
The only signs of its contents
The dark memories that steal across my soul,
Accusing me, deriding me.
You say, "Hush, love, the shadows cannot harm.
I have defeated what lies behind that door."

You hold the keys of all my life.
Teach me quiet trust
That my sins no more will chain me
Nor my future overwhelm,
That my heart will emerge victorious
Over all this world's assaults.

Storybooks
(Revelation 13, Revelation 20)

Small beginnings, storied ends,
Each generation writes a volume,
Pages filled with fidelity and fear,
Beauty and betrayal defining chapters,
Each a masterpiece of suspense.

As those tiny hands first grasp the pen
Those in the midst of their epics must teach.
How do you compose a tale that lasts?
What words touch hearts in coming ages?
What phrases ensure a place in the Book of Life?

Without our training their tales will twist.
Selfishness will stain the stories.
So we must do out part to pass on
The lessons we've learned, the tales we've lived,
Weaving their stories with ours
On the loom of laps and long car rides.
So the spoken treasure will not be forgotten.

Refugee
(Psalm 23, Psalm 84, Song of Solomon 5, Hebrews 12-13, Revelation 21)

I choose to be a refugee,
Ever wandering,
Never staying
In the crumbling castles of this world.
The hovel where I lay my head,
Where weighty trinkets often taunt,
Is temporary shelter,
Nothing more,
Save perhaps kindling for a brighter dawn.

My city, robed in righteousness,
Paves its streets with this world's gold.
Truth and faithfulness form high walls.
Angels guard the gates,
And no light shines but one true light –
The glory of the Lamb.

My feet yearn to walk those streets,
But my heart can even now tread down riches.
I long to stand upon that great high wall
And see the new earth unveiled before me,
Though even now that wall is my foundation,
And that same glorious light guides my steps.

Though homeless beneath my suburban roof,
I know my Father waits for me.
A refugee in heart and soul,
I know my Lord walks outside the camp,

Upon the burning grounds for slaughtered beasts.
My Lover has drawn me out,
Though I was dressed to slumber in the shallows,
To drown in my complacency.

There outside the camp of comforts you have built your house,
And one day there wipes clean
The very memory of any other dwelling.
Better is one day in your courts than thousands elsewhere,
And you have sworn by yourself that I, your beloved,
Would dwell in your house forever,
A spectacle of grace before my foes.

The Beauty of Mystery

Deep Magic
(Genesis 1, Romans 3, Romans 5, Hebrews 9, Revelation 5,
Chronicles of Narnia)

Pulsing in the darkness covering the earth's face,
Humming subtly like fluorescent lights in that formless
void.
If eyes had observed that primeval concoction,
Bubbling, simmering on God's great stove,
One would only notice that rhythmic dweomer by its
absence,
So enmeshed, so irrevocably one with all God planned.

Those ancient glyphs, engraved on God's hand,
Written, perhaps, in unlearned tongues
By constellations yet unseen
Reveal the fabric of the Designer's dream,
The subbest of all sub-atomic particles,
The core,
The meat,
The truth:
Treason against the Most High demands blood be spilled,
And Love has spilled his blood on our behalf,
Undoing all our sin would have wrought.

A Lion, terrible and beautiful beckons.
Whether you answer his purr or his roar is your choice,
Whether or not the paws are velveted when he takes hold
of you,
For that he will certainly do,
Depends on what you will do
Now that you have perceived the Deep Magic.

Eden to Eternity
(Genesis 2, Genesis 3, John 20, Romans 5, Hebrews 12)

What power lies within the heart,
Locked away by Adam's pride?
What wondrous flame was then snuffed out
As we joined the beasts on deathward slide?

We once were meant to rule the world,
To administer justice all around.
Our charge was to subdue and fill,
To nurture and prosper God's holy ground.

But promise transformed into pain.
A future faded into dreams
When we claimed discerning rights—
And bent our will towards selfish schemes.

Thus sin and death took up their thrones;
Toil and travail became our lot.
The earth, our womb, turned her back
Once found, now we were sought.

Where once we saw the face of glory,
We now must see it on a cross.
Where once we held the hands that formed us,
We now must first release the dross.

Yet, great mystery, it all was planned.
Every surge of pain God chose,
Each one, from Eden to eternity.
Where sin abounded grace arose.

Weeds
(Psalm 98, Isaiah 55, Romans 8, Revelation 22,
William Stafford)

William Stafford watched the weeds
Wave wildly in their dance of praise.
He heard their voice on whispering wind:
"Great is the earth our home!"
Satisfied, he stopped his ears
And missed the rest of the refrain:
"Great is the earth our home,
But greater still a home unknown!"
Though blossoms and weeds alike exult,
As mourning will it seem
When the Morning Star shines forth.

No doubt he thought the song complete.
Walking by sight, why wouldn't he?
The eyes can drink deeply at beauty's well,
But deeper still the faithful heart
That sees the Shadowlands' form

There is silk the flesh can't grasp,
A whistling wind no ear will hear.
The Spirit Realm, the Heavenlies
Defy our apprehension.

Embracing Vertigo
(Exodus 33-34, Job 40, Psalm 18, Luke 23)

You make a mockery of all my words
Simply by being you.
For though I aspire to capture you with the pen,
To contain you in the caverns of conception,
The immensity, the boundlessness, the mystery
Send my soul spiraling in the vertigo of glimpsing just
your back as you depart.
Madness lingers at the edge of the black hole of seeking
you.
Therein every pretension, every illusion is crushed;
All light by which we ourselves would search your
depths vanishes,
Snuffed, consumed by the weight of glory.
And still you draw us ever deeper, breaking us sweetly,
Stripping us of ourselves that you may emerge.
Madness to a world cold and empirical,
Incapable of trusting the unseen
Though it presses endlessly upon them,
Filling their lungs and beating their hearts.
Madness Lovecraft always longed for,
As gazing upon the unthinkable
Irrevocably changes the brave pilgrim
Whose eyes have been captured by the storm's beauty.

What terror would that abyss hold for us
Had you not bridged it yourself?
A wretched lot we are
Who cannot lay hold of that which we most need,
Our minds too small, our hearts too shriveled.

But, greatest mystery, you stepped through the
unknowable gulf of infinity
Into our time and space,
Our brokenness and weakness,
Our dust and grime and dirt and blood.
There you died,
The infinite, eternal, ineffable one
Nailed to a cross,
Dripping real blood on real earth.
A real heart stopped beating,
And real eyes closed.
Thus our sin, all too real,
All too keenly felt as we bore it to our graves
Was lifted off of us,
And life was given as that tangible stone was rolled
away.

Can I understand? Can I fathom?
Is my mind so great as to apprehend this scandal?
I place my hand over my mouth
Lest I speak untruly of you, my Lord.
I will gladly fall further into the abyss of uncertainty,
Farther from my own faculties and strength
Into the unshakable fortress of trusting you.

Obvious
(Isaiah 53, Isaiah 61, Matthew 5, Luke 2, Luke 11, Luke 22-24,
John 17, John 19, Romans 6, ICorinthians 12, Phillippians 2,
Revelation 19)

Did you catch the glory?
Wasn't it obvious in the musky air?
Didn't the blood and mess and screams
Of a newborn child make it clear as day?
Weren't the bleats and lows and clucks
A royal choir to welcome a helpless king?
Maybe the shepherds made it clearer:
Surly, shaggy, unrefined,
Sweetly perfumed with manure and old wool.

If by sheer dimness you missed it then
There were plenty more chances.
Surely you saw it in the mocking laughter
From those who construed him as a fool
Despite his noble entourage:
Thieves, harlots, lepers, fishers
Extremists, homeless, loose women.
Could the glory have been any plainer?

Let's try this one last time,
Maybe the treacherous kiss will open your eyes.
Will his bonds and beatings awaken you?
Aren't the strips of flesh flayed away magnificent?
Could the crown of thorns and regal nails
Have been any more beautiful?
Were the tearful cries of deserted Lord
Anything less than triumphant?

The slumped head, crumpled form,
And eyes rolled back in their sockets
Showed how gracious and glorious this king is.

Should you miss the glory in his humble life
You and I are much the same,
For we seek glory by gaining power
And he sought it by holding onto nothing,
Save the hearts his Father gave him.
We looked in the wrong spot for divine beauty.

So he made the glory plain at last,
To open the eyes of those who tried
With all they were to see before,
But whose weakness defeated valiant efforts.
He conquered death, our greatest foe,
As the Spirit gave life to his body,
Broken though it was.

And his body labors still
In loosing chains, restoring sight,
Unstopping ears and calling the lame to walk,
Loving enemies and dying to self.
Here the glory shines brightest,
Precursor to the sundering of all things
And establishment of Christ's righteous reign.

Higher Than Ours
(Isaiah 55, Acts 17)

Intrusive, elusive,
You shine your face into the depths of my soul
Yet remain just out of reach,
A dream's shadow.

Able, unstable,
Rock solid love and enduring faithfulness
Seamlessly woven with the whirlwind's unpredictability
That no box can hold.

Reason, treason,
Source of all I am, all joy and hope,
Fuel behind the overthrow of self,
My gentle cross.

Scandal, handle
The world-shattering truth that troubles my soul
And gives me grip on unending life,
My home is with you.

Fish Eater
(Psalm 3, Song of Solomon 2, Luke 24)

You're never where I expect you to be.
I lock you in a box and roll a stone over the opening.
I come to pay my dues with funeral spice
Because you, dead christ, are safe.

But you remove the restraining rock
And invite me into death
That I may see no box, no grave can hold you.
Living Christ you speak,
Igniting my heart to a dangerous blaze
Set to consume my comfort
As you whisper who you are to me, your enclefted dove.

You are a shield about me to ward off foes,
But no shield could I ever bring to bear
Against your reckless redeeming love.
You breathe in deep where dead me shouldn't be.
You make me marvel as you, the one the grave
swallowed,
Swallow my finest cooking.
So send your Spirit of Power
That I may bear witness to you,
Grave Breaker, Flame Bringer, Truth Speaker,
Fish Eater.
From great to small, first to last,
You are God. Amen.

Riddles
(John 3:1-21)

You speak in riddles to the fleshly mind,
Obscuring, obfuscating holy truth
That while hearing they would never know
And while seeing they would never believe.
Born again, brazen serpent, dividing light and dark,
All as fathomable as the blowing of the wind across an
arid land.

From within this entangling verbage,
This sweetly acrid blend of conflicting aromas
A clear syllable distinguishes itself,
Harmony amidst the dissonance,
Clarity amidst confusion,
An unshakable mountain of light encircled by dark clouds.
One syllable –
Love,
Unrestrained, unconditional,
The cipher to the great riddle of you,
A Living Word,
A Breathing Utterance
Adding hope to our dictionaries full of fear and sorrow.

So come blow over us inscrutably.
Though life feel momentarily like death,
Though joy may wear a tear-streaked mask,
Blow.
Rattle, rearrange, refresh,
Bring heaven to our earthly minds
That all may see your glory. Amen.

Rider With the Secret Name
(Isaiah 55, I Corinthians 1Revelation 1, Revelation 19)

Rider with the secret name,
What fire burns deep in your eyes
As you charge madly, wildly into our world,
As you brandish the glistening sword of your mouth
As you fix your gaze on your glorious bride
Adorned in righteousness for you alone?

What mystery does your name conceal?
What elusive embers of your iris' flame
Lay buried in the majesty of those syllables?
Would we see passion's inferno
Leaping from the same logs as wrathful conflagration,
Or is each fed by different hearths,
Pouring forth their fulness in due time?

Hidden deep within your heart
That secret, guarded by unapproachable light,
Dares me, taunts me
To plunge ever further into you,
Trying in vain to unravel your mystery,
You whose thoughts and ways are higher than mine,
Whose wisdom is foolishness to fleshly minds,
Whose hate is love, whose love is hate to a fallen world.
My life is death pursuing that name.

The Beauty of Consummation

Weather Forecast
(Judges 19, Matthew 5, Matthew 13, Matthew 22, Revelation 3, Revelation 9)

A broken church, a mighty church—
Mutually exclusive or one in the same?
Forecasts of latter rain dot the networks;
The promise of apostasy looms on the horizon.
Battle lines are drawn over things not yet seen.
The Body is maimed,
The woman scattered amongst the twelve tribes,
And in tribes they'll stay.
Whether unanointed or heretical,
The other camp simply won't do.

Is middle ground unwelcome compromise?
Or might there be elusive truth
Waiting to be apprehended when guards are let down?
Many are called, few chosen
But though few in number
Will their righteousness not shine like the sun?
Just because the hill-top city is visible to all
Doesn't mean they'll come streaming to it for shelter.
They may see it as a prominent target,
For we know the rest of men
Who do not die from trumpets' plagues
Will hold fast to their witchcraft and murders,
Idolatries and thefts,
Immoralities of every kind.

Could the latter rain be a localized downpour
Sent to purify a sullied Bride

While magnifying all the more the world's barrenness?
Could part of God's purpose for that glorious church
Be for shaming the many who hated her truth,
Who sought so eagerly to devour her,
Blameless though she was,
Just as they sought to consume her Groom.
Could that final church be burning coals
Heaped by their good works on the heads of deluded ones,
Used to kindle the furnace of God's wrath on a deserving world?

One truth is certain: the Lord returns
Jealous for his captive bride.

Wedding Guests
(Isaiah 53, Daniel 3, Hebrews 11, Revelation 19)

Expectant, eager, the guests await.
The ballroom doors stand motionless,
Not yet ready for the feast to begin.

The preparations are nearly done.
Refreshment has been laid out.
The guests surely need it.

Long roads were traveled for this chief of all weddings,
Painful paths through denigration and abuse,
Lonely walks through roaring flames,
Barefoot journeys across razor sharp rocks.

Nevertheless they have arrived,
Broken, rejected, despised.
The world was not worthy of them,
So he who made the world
Has prepared their place—
A seat of honor
And a balm of love.

It's All About the Bride
(Genesis 2-3, Exodus 17, I Corinthians 12, Revelation 19)

It's all about the bride:
The dress, the flowers
The registry, the cake,
Every detail made to order
Fulfilling a childhood vision.

It's all about the Bride:
Robes of righteousness made to fit
A frame no longer denying nakedness,
Budding holiness soon to bloom,
Spiritual gifts to equip the saints,
Nourishment knocked loose from stone.

It's all about the Bride
A feast prepared over millennia
Fulfilling an ancient vision
Glimpsed in a garden, clinched on a cross.

Every Nation, Every Tribe
(Isaiah 37, Isaiah 42, Revelation 7)

Invading the spectrum of art and style,
Every angle expertly attacked:
The tribal drum,
The Bedouin chant,
Two tone dronings
From secluded monasteries,
The highland's pipes,
The outback's digeridoos,
Every voice, every note
Designed in Eden to sound your praise.

Mournful dirges of ages past
Cry for comfort from your touch.
Joyous revels around the flame
Reflect the heat of your consuming love.

Each culture diverse in beauty
Finds redemption at your cross.
So every nation, tribe, and tongue
Will be heard around your throne.
No one act show,
No monocultural monotony.
You made all the nations for your pleasure.
You will be enthroned on their praise.

Aria

(Zephaniah 3, Ephesians 5, Revelation 19)

Stirred by passion, your aria begins,
A distant thunder,
Tenor for its explosive power,
Bass in its steadfast stability.
You extol your beloved's beauty,
Entranced as only a waiting Groom can be
By untarnished virtue and purity.
The melody begins slowly as you drink in her form.
You have waited for her, she for you.   .
With each sip your volume grows.
Crescendoing affection clouds the skies.
That distant thunder now erupts upon the ears of all,
An exquisite agony that pierces flesh
And reverberates within the soul's deep caverns,
Testifying unquestionably
She is loved and she is your.

Singing over her, you direct her aria.
You draw out life and earnestness,
Imbuing her performance with compelling truth,
Soprano for its scalpel-like precision
Cutting to the heart,
Alto for the haunting harmony
Of many tongues and nations singing with one voice,
The voice of the Bride.
Her aria is at once a dirge of longing
And a magnificent jubilee,
Mourning her Prince's absence
While patiently waiting his triumphant return.

Hear her words disperse as garden's fragrance:
"Holy! Holy! Holy!" is her song to you
Sung with deep conviction
And sweet desperation.

The opera ends in glory.
You ride in, blood-soaked from battle.
There is no hesitation on her part
For she, too, is washed in blood.
She runs to you; you gather her up,
The closing number an unending duet,
Redeemer and Redeemed joined in song,
Their voices making harmonic love as a marriage is consummated
Promised from the foundation of the world.

Farewells

Ignorant
(Genesis 1, Romans 8, I Peter 1)

How bad did it hurt?
What pain tormented you
That you sought to numb it with the needle's sweet venom?
I guess you wanted to feel again some day,
Just not yet,
And that lady's deadly embrace
Promised you the release you wanted,
The drug to make you think the demon pursuing you
Was just a bad dream.

Now a dream is all you are.
You traded one pain for a crueller one.
You escaped one pursuing beast,
Only to fall victim to a roaring lion
Seeking whom he may devour.
Somewhere you believed his lie
That you were worth less than you really are,
That the Maker's image was not on you,
That you were alone in a hostile world.
You believed people didn't care enough for your choices to hurt them.

For my part, I wonder,
Maybe I didn't show my love.
Maybe you couldn't receive it.
Regardless, now I shed my tears,
Cursing alternately myself and you,
Realizing that's pointless,

And, hopefully, going through the pain authentically,
Not turning back from grief's grim gate,
Nor dulling the pain of loss,
But drinking every last drop from this bitter cup.

I too have visitied dark places to hide from a fallen world,
And I know you didn't want to leave this mess behind.
I know the high obscures the consequences.
Like you, I never planned to stay for good,
But you got caught in a tighter noose than I ever did.
Now I'll help pick up the pieces with everyone else.
Maybe, just maybe, we will fashion something from
them
That will heal the wounds you never knew you made.

The Worship Leader
(Luke 15, Revelation 4)

Did you know what you delivered
Up there with your guitar and baritone?
Did you ever see just how far, how deep
The Spirit plunged into hungry hearts
As your bared your soul before your God?

Did you know how rich a crown you wrought
As you led the many to the throne
Where they could bow their hearts with yours
To glorify with unveiled eyes the living God?

And even when the music stopped
The praise went on from you,
For even in the silence the fragrance of your life
Sweetened the air of Heaven's Temple
And shone a light of hope to those still in darkness.
You knew more deeply than many
How far God's love can reach for just one sheep.
You bore the mark of that love whereever you went.

Now we all must wait a while
Before we hear again your voice of praise,
But your song we can all still hear,
Its echo reverberating through our souls
Each a little less thirsty for having known you.

Reflections From a Funeral
(I Corinthians 15)

Beauty sprouted fragrantly,
Arranged as a guardian
To ward us from death's grim glare.
"Why are these things so sad?"
Asked a mourner with a chuckling mask,
Trying to wish away the fear and pain.
Fading beauty is cause for tears,
As all which the eye beholds must one day wither.
When the eye is all that one sees with
Then the sorrow is inescapable.
Sin's curse shall make dust of all we cling to,
Leaving us empty,
Barren.

The real question we dare not even whisper.
"What will be my final fate
When earth or flame consume my flesh,
Or when some other greedy maw
Locks away my tent eternally?"

When we grasp the searing truth,
When we face the crass nakedness of death
Do we despair
Or find in the emptiness
A space at last for Christ to fill,
Whose severe mercy awakens us from deadly slumber,
Takes the burdens we love so much
And leaves us only himself to cling to?

Old Glory
(Deuteronomy 28, I Kings 18, Zechariah 14, IICorinthians 3)

Old Glory flutters in the breeze,
Symbol of a proud people,
Idol of a nation turned away.
No longer do I love those colors.
The red stinks too much of others' blood.
The blue reminds me of the ghastly hue
Consuming the face of the strangled poor.
The white suggests the pallor of dead hearts.
The nation's glory is old and withered.

I still wish Old Glory well
As one wishes well a feebleminded old fool
Pitifully dying in a neglected hospice.
I wish there were more I could do,
But the end is inevitable.
Old glory fades away.

What will become of those
Who have not found a new glory,
A lasting glory that will not fail?
Nothing left to do but lift high the rotting corpse
Of a nation long dead
And dance and cut in vain hope that the dead will
breathe.
The stench deepens.
The blood keeps flowing.
Death gives birth to all it can,
More death.

Goodbye
(Psalm 133, Romans 8, Ephesians 5, Revelation 2,
Revelation 7, Revelation 20)

The work is done and parting is near.
Do bonds formed in love's crucible
Endure past the last glimpse from rearview mirrors?
Does the incense offered as night deepened
Linger like a dream in the cabins of vans and airplanes
Bound for far corners of a lonely land?
Will fellowship's sweet oil truly bear us home
To the arms of our one Father and our beloved Co-heir?
Will the Spirit knit and bind mysteriously
Hearts that may never meet again
Till books are opened and the dead are judged?

The distance, the time make it hard to believe,
But rest assured we will meet there,
Along with every nation, tribe, and tongue,
Giving glory to our Bridegroom, our First Love
With one voice,
With one heart.
So hold on to hope of family reunited.

Dedications and Distractions

Convenient Love
(John 3, I Corinthians 13, Phillippians 2)

You've had it all your life, I guess:
The kind of love that uses you,
Convenient love that bends only so far,
Enough to live at peace.
It's really no love at all.
Those objects (fitting word) of conveneint love
Cannot themselves love recklessly,
Thoughtless of the dangers ahead,
Heedless of impending storms,
Yet ever contemplating the beloved,
Not to fill obsessive needs
Nor to satiate unwholesome fascination
But simply, purely for the buried beauty
In a hurting soul interred by foolish choices.

You need no more convenient love;
You need no safe and casual care.
Your homes, your gangs have quite enough;
For there love falters when costs are counted.
Come taste a reckless love from heart to heart.
Come see through eyes that do not flinch
When love demands great sacrifice.
Torment and death lay before such love
And yet it persevered to the end,
To the cross,
And so shall I, if God be pleased.
I will love you recklessly.
Thus my pledge is written,
And, prayerfully, will it be lived.
You shall find in me the love of Christ.

Daughter of Zion
(Exodus 15, Ruth 1, Psalm 84, Zephaniah 3)

Has famine sent you far from home,
To Moab where no love is known?
Has fear consumed your hopes and dreams,
Entangled you in Satan's schemes?

Daughter of Zion, hear this word:
Though his appearing be deferred,
The Lord still stands beside your soul.
With songs of love he shall console.

He is a warrior, King of kings,
And though much pain this darkness brings,
With glory will you be adorned
As he brings victory with the morn.

Walk through weeping's looming vale;
Let him hear your fearful wails.
He draws out all within your heart
So that he may himself impart.

In that vale shall springs burst forth,
Cooling, quenching, love their source.
From strength to strength you will endure,
Daughter of Zion, washed so pure.

To be Wooden and Woolen
(I Corinthians 13, Ephesians 5)

It's a cold, dark night out there,
But it's not much better in here.
We'd chop wood for a fire
But our ax-heads are rusted.
We'd wrap ourselves in woolen blankets
But we've worn too many holes in them.
No chance to huddle close to feel a warm body;
The walls are still a bit too high.
My heart would see love flow from me to you,
But affection's arteries are clogged with callousness.
The desire to gaze with transparent eyes and glowing
face tears me apart
Because I can't. Not yet, not now.
"I need to change," I tell you, and I really mean it.
"I'll be content to watch it," you say with your own
wellspring eyes.
Do you wonder what that does to me?
Do you wonder how I receive those words leavened with
love?
They smash me to pieces and grind me to dust
Because I can't be those logs or that blanket,
And neither can you.

You in the clouds, who sends the rain,
The rain that washes away my world,
That washes away my sin,
Why can't I love her like I know I should?
Look from your throne and behold this wretch
Whose flesh is too much for his holy desires.

Wash away those walls. They're made from the same dust as I.

"You will be content to watch? Then so will I be.
I'll watch as my holes are sewn up
And my coals are stoked and fueled.
Then I will wrap you in me and keep you warm,
And I will give you light, however dim.
For the same has been done for me so many times before,
And I can't bear keeping it from you."

Cleaving
(Song of Solomon 4)

Sweet are the delicacies you keep for me.
Intoxicating the wine you pour in secret.
Sparkling the stones only I may see.
Soft is your flower bed, shaming velvet.

Delicious, delicate is the fruit you bear.
Too firmly grasped and the fruit will bruise.
So gently I pluck each morsel rare.
Your flowing nectar my strength renews.

Unlike any feast is this lovers' repose,
Captured only in part with honeyed pen.
Yet even more fragrant than this sheltered rose
Is your soul's secret garden deep within.

So swing wide the gates, there I will rest
After working the soil with tender hands.
Not upon but behind your two perfect breasts,
There is my fountain, my fertile land.

I'll cultivate my land with gentleness,
Removing rocks and thorns the world has sown,
Guarding my land against barrenness,
For you are flesh of my flesh, bone of my bone.

Listen
(Proverbs 10)

Love bites its tongue when words are raw,
Intent upon communicating gentleness,
Soothing first with eyes and heart,
Then, much later, with thoughtful words,
Elegantly wrapped as gauze upon a wound.
No scars left, only character.